BETTER ARCHERY

E.G. HEATH

BETTER ARCHERY

with 100 illustrations

KAYE & WARD · LONDON
in association with Hicks, Smith & Sons
New Zealand and Australia

First published in Great Britain by
Kaye & Ward Limited
21 New Street, London EC2M 4NT
1976

I S B N 0 7182 1446 3

Filmset in Monophoto Times by Keyspools Limited, Golborne, Lancs
Printed in Great Britain by Whitstable Litho, Whitstable, Kent

Contents

Acknowledgements

The author's grateful thanks are extended to S. E. Crisp, Secretary of the Association for Archery in Schools, for his initial encouragement for this project, and to Ellis Shepherd, National Coaching Organiser, Grand National Archery Society, for his constructive comments on the text.

Acknowledgements are also due to the Grand National Archery Society from whose *Rules of Shooting* several extracts have been taken, and to D. G. Quick of Bishop Bros (Hampshire) Ltd who kindly allowed reproduction of illustrations on page 10.

The majority of the photographs were specially taken by David Manners with the help of Sharon Smith, Stephen Jones, Raymon Dawes, Gary Taylor and Mike Driscoll, who acted as willing models and whose patient co-operation is greatly appreciated. Mark Davis of the Association for Archery in Schools and the Canterbury Archers kindly provided facilities for these photographs. The remainder of the illustrations are provided by the author.

Author's Note
Measurements are given sometimes in imperial and sometimes in metric in accordance with whatever rules are being quoted, G.N.A.S. or F.I.T.A.

Foreword

Archery is a very personal sport and the degree of individual success depends on the amount of practice – both mental and physical – which the archer is able to devote to it. It is a sport which is continually increasing in popularity, and in which all members of the family can, and do, take part, at times competing side by side under the same conditions.

This book will help both beginners and more accomplished archers to achieve their own personal level of success.

Ellis Shepherd
National Coaching Organiser
Grand National Archery Society

The Right Equipment

Many of the points made in this introductory chapter may be considered superfluous by those who have already taken up the bow. Nonetheless they should be carefully considered as a checklist of the more important factors which are essential if any progress is to be made in the sport. It is fruitless and frustrating trying to improve if the faults lie in the equipment and not the archer. There is much truth in the saying, 'When the arrow fits the bow and the bow fits the archer, the perfect shot is made'. All too often aspiring beginners, disheartened by an apparent inability to improve, have given up archery altogether, whereas by following a few simple guidelines they would have had the chance, if not the satisfaction, of making that 'perfect shot'. The best archers are those who seek to improve their own performance; it is a very individual challenge and one which requires personal discipline. Archery is a satisfying pursuit. It can be relaxing and exhilarating at the same time, and the development of the co-ordination between physical activity and mental concentration results from following a prescribed routine, a task both absorbing and rewarding.

BOWS

One inevitable topic of discussion amongst archers concerns the bows and arrows they use. Whether they be novices who have recently taken up the sport or experts who have reached international standards, whenever they meet they will talk of the relative merits of one type of bow compared with others, the intricacies of design, performance, and the many details of the great variety of 'tackle' that is now available. The finer technical points may bewilder the uninitiated, but the basic fact which prompts such discussion is, in brief, the search for the best equipment for the individual.

Let us start with the premise that no two people are alike. This being the case, it is reasonable to assume that the ideal bow and arrows for one person are not

9

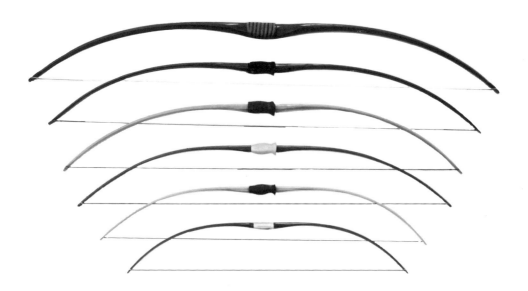

A range of solid fibre-glass bows which includes flat bows (*top*) and recurve bows (*bottom*). Sizes and weights vary according to the physique of the archer. Recurve bows are more efficient than flat bows.

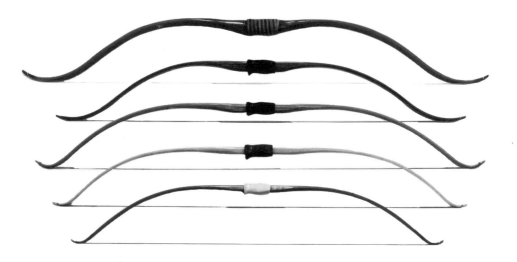

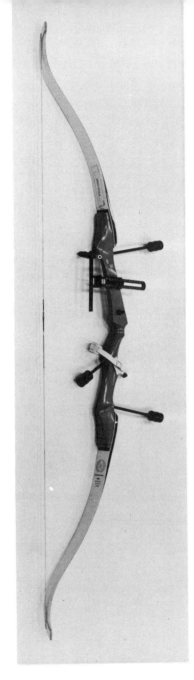

Two composite bows of advanced design. The bow on the left has detachable limbs, twin stabilizers and counter-balance system, and a side mounted sight. The bow on the right is equipped with a single stabilizer and counter-balance.

necessarily the best for someone else. The catalogues issued by the archery suppliers list a very wide choice of equipment, but of course there are limitations to the exclusiveness of archery tackle produced commercially. What is important at the outset for the individual is for him, or her, to make a selection of the most suitable equipment, and this choice is governed by one or two simple facts.

There is a wide price range of bows and arrows now available, and the novice would be well advised to consider using a solid fibre-glass bow for practice until he or she is confident enough to invest in more expensive equipment. More advanced bows are made to more critical standards, and a good archer will reap the benefit of buying the best he can afford. For beginners, however, and even for those who have had some experience in shooting, fibre-glass bows properly used can produce some excellent results.

The bow should be suited to the height and strength of the archer. All bows are measured by the weight in pounds that have to be exerted to draw arrows of specified lengths. This is not as complicated as it sounds, for example, a beginner's bow may be listed as drawing 28 lb at 28 in., although shorter arrows could be used in the same bow, in which case they would require less poundage to draw them fully. The choice of the weight of the bow is critical, because using a bow too strong to be comfortably handled, that is by being 'overbowed', will prove disastrous in developing a good performance. The advice of a qualified club instructor or coach is recommended as the simplest and surest way of deciding on the best choice of a bow.

The parts of a bow. The flat surface which faces the archer is called the 'belly' and the opposite surface is called the 'back' of the bow.

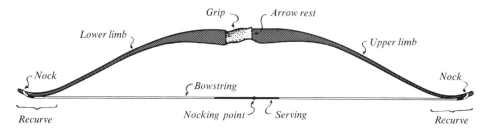

12

Shaft   Fletchings

Pile   Cresting   Nock

The parts of an arrow. Fletchings can vary in shape and may be made of plastic or real feathers. The 'cock' feather is always set at right-angles to the 'nock' or string slot. The cresting, in various colours, identifies the owner.

ARROWS

The same advice applies equally to the selection of arrows, which must be the correct length and must match the bow in their weight, and in their stiffness or 'spine'. Manufacturers usually recommend the correct spine-rating and weight to match the bow of your choice. The length of arrows is all-important and, although a novice can shoot well enough with arrows a little too long for him, once he has become more proficient, the arrow length must be carefully selected to suit his particular physique. A satisfactory initial method of calculating a suitable arrow length is to hold an arrow between the hands held together at arms' length extended in front of the body, with one end of the arrow placed high on the breast bone.

A selection of arrows. From the top: popinjay arrow, wooden field arrow, fibre-glass field arrow, target arrow of fibre-glass, 28in. alloy target arrow, steel target arrow, 26in. target arrow.

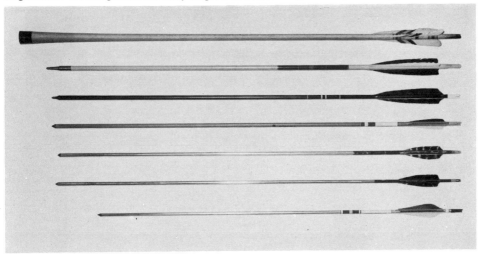

13

The elementary check for a suitable arrow length. On no account must arrows be used that are too short. A more detailed measurement must be taken when the archer is more proficient.

ACCESSORIES

Two other essentials are required: a shooting tab and a bracer. The shooting tab comprises a flat, smooth, leather protector for the fingers of the shooting hand, which enables the release of the string to be made as smoothly as possible. As an alternative, a shooting glove can be used, which usually consists of leather finger stalls attached to a skeleton glove fastened at the wrist. Whichever article is used, the function is the same. The tab or glove is a very personal piece of equipment and must fit properly to be effective. Many varieties of design are available commercially, but archers frequently prefer to make their own tabs from a tough pliable leather known as pony crupp butt. Time taken to ensure that the tab fits exactly will pay dividends.

The tab (*above left*) is of conventional pattern: (*below left*) a tab with a finger spacer. The shooting glove can be used as an alternative finger protection.

Various types of bracers. A number of other types are available and the choice is determined by comfort and practicality.

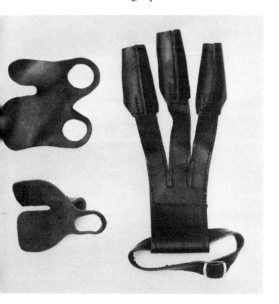

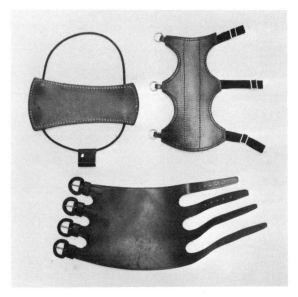

The bracer consists of a protective leather or plastic guard strapped to the left forearm (when the bow is held in the left hand). The released bow-string can foul loose sleeves and sometimes chaff the arm, and the bracer ensures that nothing hinders the string's forward movement. There is a psychological gain for the novice who wears a bracer, because he is not worried about the possibility of a bruised forearm – however, if the bow is held properly, such a problem does not arise.

Other accessories, although not absolutely necessary, which invariably form part of the archer's tackle include a quiver, a ground quiver, and a tassel. The quiver is normally slung from the waist belt and hangs at a convenient angle, so that arrows temporarily stored there are readily accessible. It can be a simple

The correct use of a ground quiver. This one is home-made, constructed of white-painted metal rod. The bow is fibre-glass.

There are no restrictions as to the type of quiver used. Note the tassel made of thick woollen strands in club colours for which there is an optional central register to prevent duplication.

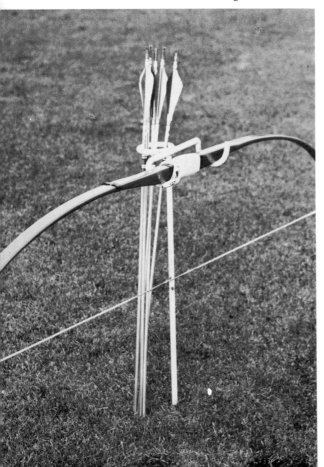

tube or an elaborate work of leather-craft according to the fancy of the individual. The ground quiver can be stuck into the ground providing a convenient means of resting the bow and storing the arrows whilst the archer waits his turn to shoot. This simple gadget plays an important part not only in the tidyness of the shooting ground but also in preventing damage to bows and arrows otherwise left carelessly lying around. The tassel represents both tradition and utility. Originally designed to be used to wipe wet or dirty arrows, it has become rather more of an ornament by being made in club colours.

MAINTENANCE

Regular maintenance of an archer's equipment ensures that it is always in good condition and safe to use. A loose feather or a frayed string can result in erratic shooting as well as a bad temper. Before and after every shooting session it is a good habit to check your tackle. See that all fletchings are secure, make sure that no arrows are bent, check the string for fraying, and ensure that the serving and nocking points are intact. When not in use, store your equipment neatly and safely. Minor do-it-yourself repairs, which are invariably carried out as routine or in an emergency, can easily be picked up by seeking the advice of other archers. It is a matter of common sense and practicability rather than specially acquired skills which enable the most inexperienced archer to cope admirably in looking after his own tackle.

Once the correct equipment has been chosen with a little forethought and guidance, a routine based on sound principles of shooting can begin. Many aspiring archers, who have begun to shoot with casually acquired bows and arrows, experience disappointment in their own inability to progress. The more they practise, possibly on their own or with non-specialist guidance, the less successful they become, and in a short while the bows and arrows are discarded for other pursuits. Often initial faults which remain uncorrected become habitual and the novice becomes disheartened. There is no easy way to good shooting, but by following well-tried methods good shooting is made easier.

THE ARCHER'S VISION

We tend to take for granted the part played by the vision of the archer. Without this faculty there would, of course, be no archery. An understanding of the importance of the optical functions and the accompanying problems of aiming will make all the difference between accurate shooting and inconsistency.

When a sight is taken, with an arrow at full draw, both eyes can be open, or the disengaged eye can be closed. In either case only one eye is used: the one known as the dominant or controlling eye. With very few exceptions, everyone can easily check which is their dominant eye. Hold both hands out in front of you at arm's length, and form a peephole with the thumbs and fingers about $1\frac{1}{2}$ in. across, and look at a distant object through the opening. Now without moving your head, close one eye and then the other. Whichever eye still sees the distant object through the opening is your dominant eye. This eye, doing your sighting for you, is naturally of the utmost importance. A right-handed person (the bow held in the left hand) whose *left* eye is dominant is going to have some difficulty

Checking the dominant eye: (*left*) the view with both eyes open; (*right*) the view with the *right* or dominant eye closed. (The image would appear on the right if the left eye is dominant and is closed.)

in shooting, because the visual phenomenon which takes place makes it impossible to line up accurately sight, arrow and target, and any corrections in aiming will be offset by this optical falsity. For those who have difficulty in this respect, the handling of the bow must be reversed in the very early stages of shooting. Provided the archer is aware of which eye is dominant and shoots left or right-handed accordingly, it will be found advantageous to practise shooting with both eyes open – this will allow the dominant eye to take over.

For reasons of clarity, *all the information given in the following chapters is for right-handed archers*, where the bow is held in the left hand, with the right eye dominant. The question of aiming is most important and this is discussed fully in chapter 5.

When the aim is taken with both eyes open, the dominant eye takes over, thus avoiding the distraction of having to close one eye.

Standing

There is no formal method of shooting which *must* be followed. It may well be that some archers have succeeded in achieving a reasonable proficiency by self-taught methods, or by emulating one of the many schools of shooting. However, a great deal of time and effort by trained coaches and instructors has resulted in the emergence of what is known as the Basic Method. This is to be commended both as a satisfactory system for teaching beginners and as a set of techniques which forms the basis for more advanced archers to improve their performance. Individuals often introduce variations to the Basic Method; there is no harm in that – provided the results pay off in terms of better shooting. However, when changes, no matter how small, appear to make no difference to your shooting, it is time to go back to basics. In fact, it is a good rule, applicable to both novices and the more experienced, to review regularly your own shooting techniques in accordance with the Basic Method. The chapters that follow incorporate the Basic Method together with supplementary notes for progressive archery.

THE SHOOTING LINE

Shooting distances are carefully measured and they vary according to the round being shot, or they are set at distances for practice purposes, 30 to 40 yards being convenient for the latter, to begin with. The shooting line is indicated by marking a white line on the grass or by a tape. The archer stands with one foot each side of this line and at right angles to it, the feet being placed a comfortable distance apart, the recommended distance being about the same width as the shoulders. The weight of the body should be distributed evenly on both feet and the archer should stand upright but not rigid, relaxed and alert. Adjustment of this position is essential until the shoulders are aligned in such a way that an imaginary straight line drawn through them is directed towards the target or aiming mark. This can be checked simply. Look straight ahead with arms outstretched level with your shoulders and, with your left eye closed (assuming that your right eye is dominant), turn your head to the left and look at the target.

If you can see that your outstretched left arm, the bow arm, is pointing directly at the target then all is well. If not then move your feet slightly until the right position has been established. It is worthwhile taking care to check this position each time you shoot until you are confident that you are standing correctly. The direction of a line drawn through the feet in relation to the shoulder line is of minimal importance, so long as you stand in a relaxed and comfortable position. Once a satisfactory stance has been taken, the position of each foot can be fixed by the use of foot markers, which can remain until the end of a practice session or round. The reason for the particular care that must be taken to establish the correct shooting position will become clear when actual shooting begins.

The basic body position. The targets are set at the appropriate distance on a line parallel to the clearly marked shooting line.

Taking up the correct alignment. The arms and shoulders should now be in direct line with the target.

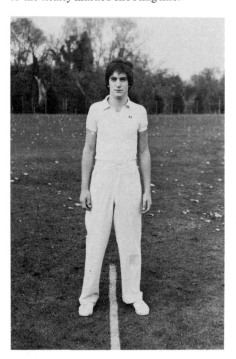

The overall aim when shooting in a bow, particularly in Target Shooting, is to achieve absolute consistency of position, movement and timing for every individual shot. It is through a conscious effort to achieve consistency that the basis of good shooting is established. With practice many of the necessary preliminary aspects can be performed automatically, but even the best archers find from time to time that they have to review critically their shooting style. A bad habit is hard to break, it is easier to get it right to begin with until it becomes second nature.

It is important to remember that the head must turn without tilting, and the view is taken with the dominant eye. For a left-handed archer the position will be reversed.

Once a satisfactory stance has been taken, the position of each foot can be fixed by the use of foot markers, which must not exceed 1cm. in height and which can remain whilst the archer is shooting.

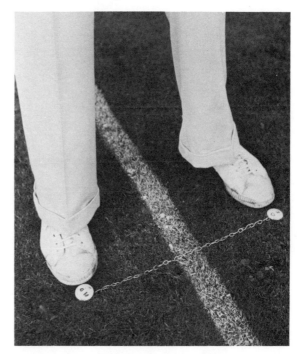

BODY POSITION

Once the correct stance has been taken, the whole process of shooting relies on several distinct and controlled physical movements. It is worthwhile considering these:

1. Keep the head upright and do not tilt it sideways or backwards when it is turned towards the target.

2. Shoulders should be kept horizontal and in line with the target.

3. All movements which lift and draw the bow are controlled by arm and back muscles.

4. The final alignment of the bow at full draw is made by a minimal movement of the upper body from the waist.

All these points will be discussed in greater detail in later chapters, but it is as well that these principles are understood from the beginning.

Bracing recurved bows by taking the tension across the back of the left leg and the front of the right. The right hand holds the string ready to slip into place. Care should be taken not to twist the bow.

The method for bracing self-wood or fibre-glass bows. Pull back the bow with the right hand, at the same time push with the left hand and slip the string loop in place in the upper nock. Gently relax the tension.

A popular method of bracing composite bows by means of a 'bow stringer', which is a secondary, detachable string held under the foot. By pulling the bow upwards the proper bow string loop can be located in its nock.

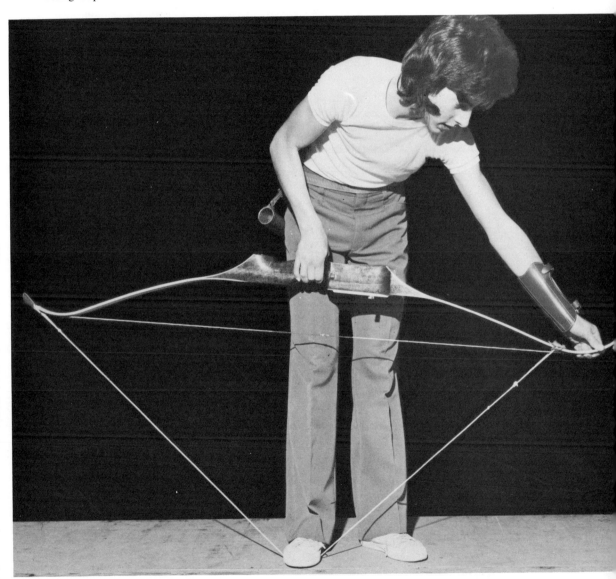

HOLDING THE BOW

Having established the way the stance should be taken, it is time to check that the bow is held correctly. Hold the bow with the arm downwards and with the string uppermost. A good method of ensuring that the hand is correctly positioned is first to extend your thumb along the centre of the face of the bow – this will ensure that your fingers are neither too far round the handgrip, nor insufficiently so – now, close your thumb round the handgrip. Do not grip the bow tightly, nor use too feeble a grasp; a controlled grip without tension is ideal. Raise your bow arm to shoulder level with the bow horizontal to the ground, then turn your hand from the wrist so that the bow is exactly vertical. Do not twist your arm. If this is done properly, the elbow of your bow arm will point outwards and not downwards. Flex your elbow joint slightly so that your arm curves away gently from the string. If there is a gap between the string and your arm then a good position has been achieved. There is a sound reason for this which relates to the necessity of allowing the bow-string free passage once it has been released. If attention is not paid to the position of the bow arm as we have described it, undue tension in the arm can produce a sideways jerking of the bow, and there is the danger of the string fouling the sleeve or arm, throwing the arrow off course. Do not, therefore, lock the elbow of your bow arm.

The bow should be held as we have described it throughout shooting; too tight a grip can cause bad shooting. Additionally, remember that the bow must remain vertical. A bow canted to left or right, even slightly, will throw arrows to right or left respectively. When the bow is under tension, i.e. at full draw, the pressure exerted by your bow hand must be evenly distributed. This is the reason why correct positioning of your bow hand is important. Extra pressure to the right or left of the bow handle or too much pressure at the base of your hand will result in arrows going off course.

The excellent fibre-glass bows of moderate cost, which are recommended for less advanced shooting, are provided with little or no shaping of the hand grip. Composite bows, which are universally popular with archers, invariably incorporate sculptured hand grips. The contours of these bow handles are varied in shape and have been devised as a result of field trials by archer-bowyers. The essential feature in all these shapes is that the choice should not only provide comfort but it should also accommodate the hand so that an even and direct pressure on the bow can be applied.

The first stage of the exercise by which a good bow position can be attained.

Preliminary position for the correct hold on a bow. Keep your wrist straight.

Now close your thumb, and this will ensure that the hand pressure is evenly balanced.

The arm and wrist are kept straight and the body position should not change.

Turn your hand only from the wrist until the bow is vertical. Your arm should not be twisted and the elbow of your bow arm should not be locked.

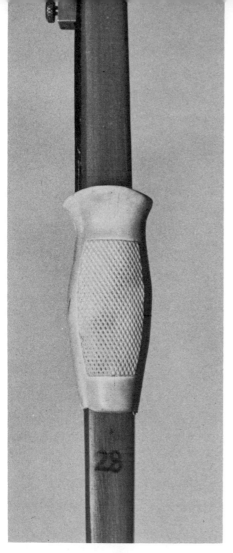

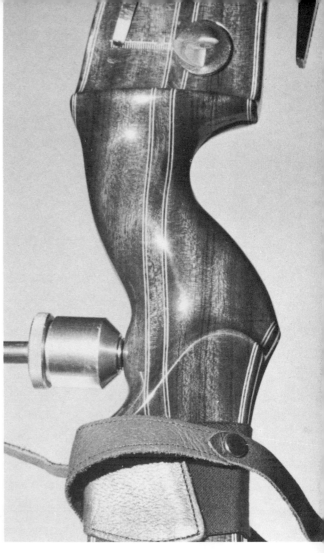

A side view of the simple hand grip of a fibre-glass bow. The top part of the moulded grip forms an arrow shelf.

A typical sculptured hand grip of a composite bow which provides a more individual method of holding a bow.

For the beginner there is a lot to remember, and for the archer with some experience who wants to improve there are many matters to re-examine. For all archers who seek better scores none of these matters are elementary – they are vital and should be constantly reviewed.

31

The bow held ready for nocking as the archer selects his arrow.

Drawing

NOCKING THE ARROW

Having taken up the correct stance, the arrow is now nocked on to the string and, like everything else in archery, it is best to carry out this simple task in a regular fashion. There are several ways in which this can be carried out, but the method which has found the most favour in recent years can be briefly described. The bow is held horizontally in front of the body with the string towards you. Take an arrow from the quiver or ground quiver between the thumb and forefinger of your right hand and lay it across the bow against the arrow rest. Making sure that the cock feather is uppermost, draw the arrow back and carefully engage the nock with the nocking point of the string.

Other methods of nocking can be equally efficient but, whatever method you choose to adopt, you must ensure that the arrow is nocked at exactly the same

Engaging the nock on the string. The arrow should be at right-angles to the string in exactly the same position each time.

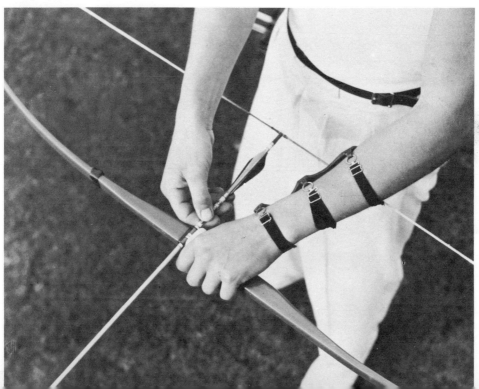

spot each time and check that the cock feather is at right angles to the string, away from the bow.

THE PREPARATION POSITION

Now place the three fingers of your right hand, the 'shaft' hand, in position on the string, one above and two below the arrow (see illustration on page 35). A correct initial position facilitates a smooth and steady draw. The string should lie across the crease of the first joints of the fingers and the forefinger should lightly touch the arrow. The hand must be flat and the wrist must be straight.

When the bow is drawn, the angle formed by the string becomes more acute and there is a tendency for fingertips and arrow nock to become pinched

An alternative method of nocking, where the arrow is passed under the bow and the nock end is brought back towards the string and pushed home on the nocking point.

Whatever method of nocking is employed, it is essential that the arrow nock is pushed gently but firmly right home on the nocking point, and the arrow should remain in this position by the snugness of its fit.

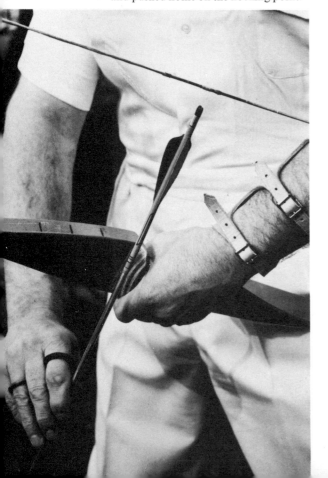

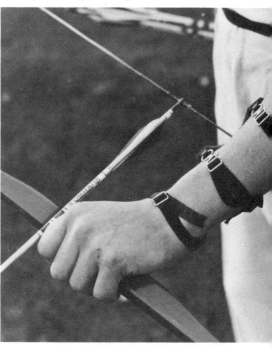

together; apart from being painful, this deflects the arrow on release, so to compensate for this a slight gap is allowed between arrow and fingers. We recommend that you leave about $\frac{1}{8}$in. gap between your second finger and the arrow.

Now gently take up the tension of the string, adjusting your final hand position whilst under slight tension. Keeping your fingers in place, let the string go back to its normal position and check that the arrow and drawing arm are exactly in line, and remain so throughout the sequence of shooting. This is known as the Preparation Line. When you are confident that everything so far is as it should be, clear your mind of extraneous thoughts and with body poised, not tense, and above all comfortable, turn your head towards the target. You are now in what is described as the Preparation Position.

How the fingers are placed on the string. Note that the hand is flat and that there is a small gap between the middle finger and the arrow to obviate pinching. The fletchings are plastic.

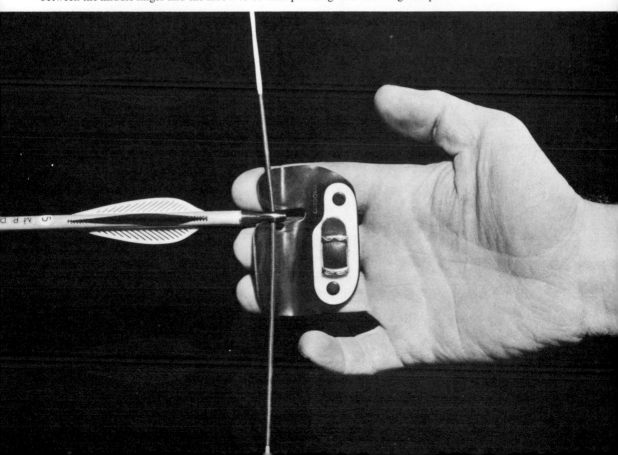

The Preparation Line, where the arrow and the drawing arm are in a straight line.

The Preparation Position immediately before the bow is drawn.

Below: Addressing the target; poised for the draw in the Preparation Position.

A limited draw used to shoot arrows into the ground for preliminary loosing practice.

Right: The first attempt at loosing. Note that the fingers are straightened, the bow is held in position and the string is clear of the bracer.

PRELIMINARY PRACTICE

Before proceeding to the all-important drawing of the arrow, it may prove helpful to recall advice given to beginners at this stage to help them appreciate the operation of shooting, without the effort of drawing the bow fully. It is a good idea to shoot some arrows into the ground a few yards away. Do this by drawing the bow back a short distance, pause for a moment, and then draw back another inch or so at the same time straightening the fingers of the shaft hand. This is the 'loose' and, when you have got the hang of it, you will have some idea of the movement that is necessary to loose an arrow at full draw. Two simultaneous movements are involved: straightening the fingers, and moving the hand backwards continuing the direction of the Preparation Line.

38

The first method of drawing the bow. From the Preparation Position the bow is turned to a vertical full draw position in one smooth movement. The Preparation Line is maintained throughout, the shoulders should be kept level, and the body position remains static.

FULL DRAW

From the Preparation Position it is now time to come to full draw. There are several ways in which this can be achieved and one of those most generally used is as follows. It is best done with the two hands pushing and pulling respectively, extending the bow and string, at the same time bringing the bow to a vertical position with bow arm fully extended, and drawing back the shaft arm until the first finger touches you just beneath the jaw. The whole action must be done smoothly and fairly smartly, without jerking.

The Preparation Line, which involves keeping arrow and shaft arm in a straight line, must be maintained throughout the draw and in the final position at full draw. The action is not performed solely with your fingers and arms. It should feel as though your shoulder muscles, right across the back, are doing the work and that they are 'using' your arms and fingers as levers and hooks, until your shoulder-blades come together. At full draw the string should just touch the centre of your nose and chin, but on no account must it touch your chest. This is the ideal and recommended arrangement, and, if there is any difficulty in getting this right, a slight tilting forward of the head may be the answer. During the whole sequence of drawing, you should not move your body.

40

A second method of drawing consists of raising the bow until the bow hand is approximately level with the top of the head, the upper part of the bow arm being in the full draw position. The shaft hand should be about six inches clear of the face with the nock of the arrow about level with the mouth. Bring the bow hand down, at the same time extending the bow to full draw.

42

Another method of drawing starts with the bow held upright with the bow arm slightly bent. Draw back the string at the same time pushing the bow forward to full draw position. No matter what method of drawing is used, the final position that is assumed must be consistent.

It may be easier for beginners to practise drawing the bow without an arrow to get the feel of what is, to most, an unaccustomed movement. Do not, however, release the string without an arrow in the bow, as a 'dry release' can be harmful to the bow.

Right: Remember the position of the bow arm: slightly flexed with the elbow pointing outwards and not downwards. Try to achieve 'controlled relaxation', the elbow must not be locked in a rigid position, and the wrist and shoulders should not be taut.

46

THE ANCHOR

The 'anchor point' is the position to which the forefinger of the shaft hand is drawn, underneath the centre of the chin, and it is to this point that the arrow must be drawn precisely each time a shot is made. This will bring the Line of Sight and the Line of Flight into their correct relationship. To maintain the same distance between anchor point, string, and eye is an important matter.

A positive and clear anchor point must be achieved each time an arrow is drawn. Note the flat hand and straight wrist.

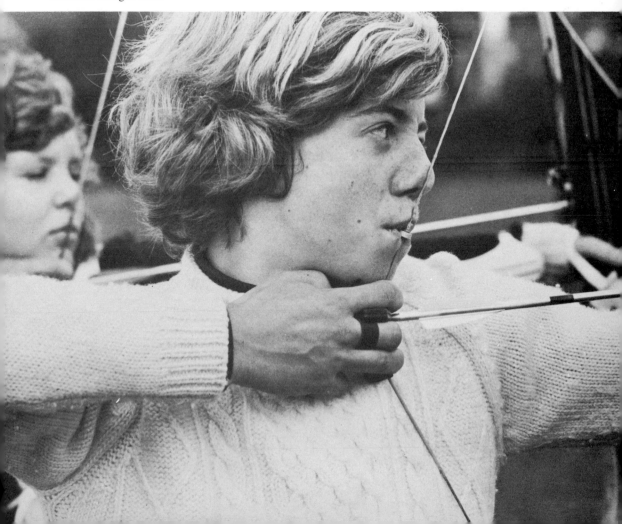

INDIVIDUAL DISCIPLINE

Drawing is the beginning of the sequence of shooting. From the moment the archer begins this movement there is only one escape from conscious errors. It happens, occasionally, even with champions, that a slight fault in drawing back the arrow, which could mar an otherwise perfect shot, is realised in time. Then the archer must let down his bow, replace the arrow in the quiver, take up the Preparation Position, clear his mind and start again. Try to discipline yourself mentally to check all the finer points of the act of shooting as the action unfolds; it will very soon become relatively automatic. If there appears to be something not quite right, start again and give yourself time to think of what might have gone wrong, and correct it the second time.

Archery is not a hurried sport, and the mental process is as important as the physical effort. Horace Ford, twelve times British Champion, said of drawing, 'On the manner in which it is accomplished very much depends: not only the ease and grace of the entire performance but also the accuracy and certainty of the hitting.' He added, 'Nothing but constant and unremitting practice will serve the archer here.' The first point he made is very interesting. If the best archers are studied, you will invariably notice that their movements follow a regular rhythm, not necessarily the same for each archer, but nevertheless discernible as an individually acquired pattern, which never varies. Anything done well is a pleasure to watch. Develop your own shooting rhythm by perfecting each individual stage of the whole sequence, linking them together in a pattern which can be repeated consistently, and the accuracy and certainty of hitting will follow.

Holding

THE PAUSE

Once the bow has been fully drawn, there is a pause during which the aim is fixed. It is also a convenient moment for the archer to make a rapid assessment of the correctness of every point which has to be observed to enable him to accomplish the task ahead successfully.

The many details which have been explained so far, if not done properly, will affect the final stages of the shooting sequence. It is at the moment of pause, when the bow is held fully drawn, that a number of faults may be recognised. It is much easier to see these faults in others and to ask someone, who knows what to look for of course, to watch your shooting can be a great help.

As a useful alternative the beginner is recommended to get the feel of the final pose at full draw, preferably with dummy equipment, in front of a mirror. This is an ideal procedure to check your own stance, hand and arm positions, shoulders and so on. Let us repeat the most important matters to watch for. The shaft arm and arrow must still be in line – remember the Preparation Line. The distance the arrow is drawn must be constant. This can only be achieved by reaching forward with the bow arm, slightly flexed, to exactly the same extent every time an arrow is drawn, and by drawing back the shaft arm to anchor at precisely the same spot. No movement forward or backward of either hand must be allowed.

The position of the arrow point in relation to the eye must remain constant, both vertically and horizontally – do not tilt your head sideways. Any vertical alteration in the distance between your eye and the position of the anchor point, even a fraction of an inch, will be multiplied by the time the arrow reaches its destination. Pay attention to both hands. They should be balanced, that is to say they must not be twisted in relation to each other. The shaft hand should remain flat, the fingers should be straight and not slanted. Make sure that the pressure on the bow handle is evenly distributed and maintain this throughout shooting. Do not grip the bow too tightly. See that the bow is not canted to left or right, or tilted backwards or forwards.

The pause is a critical moment during which the whole action so far should be reviewed. The breath should be held with lungs normally filled throughout the whole sequence. It is the bow that is held in balance at full draw and not the arrow. An imaginary line, sometimes called the Draw Force Line, follows a path through the elbow of the drawing arm, the nock of the arrow and the pressure point of the hand on the bow.

Many archers have experienced the irritation of the arrow falling off the arrow shelf once the bow has been drawn. This can occur if the drawn arrow is pinched between the fingers, or if the shaft hand and bow hand are out of line or twisted in relation to each other.

How long should the bow be held at full draw in the aiming position? This is a very personal matter, and the pause varies according to the archer. Some archers take what appears to be a considerable time before finally loosing the arrow, whereas others are brief. When shooting a round, under the rules of the Grand National Archery Society, a limit of two and a half minutes is allowed for an archer to shoot three arrows, from the time he steps on to the shooting line.

ATTENTION TO DETAIL

All these matters may seem to be a lengthy catalogue of 'remember this' and 'don't forget that', but they are important and each point, if it is not done properly, will produce a shooting error. These are essential aspects of technique which are worth studying, because once the arrow has left the bow its direction is pre-determined, and the result of bad technique can never be changed. Far better to ensure that, by developing a good technique, you are doing everything possible to shoot the arrow as accurately as it can be shot. The course of the arrow entirely depends on the climax of physical control on release. Thus any factor which interferes with the proper management of the pause should be thoroughly investigated and dealt with. So long as the whole sequence is controlled by conscious effort no problems arise. Good scores, and personal satisfaction, begin with careful attention to these matters.

Young archers in action on the shooting line at the Association for Archery in Schools, Inter-Team Shoot, at Beckenham in October 1975.

Aiming

For those who have learnt the rudiments of archery and who have started to shoot, there is a temptation to get arrows in the general direction of the target without carefully considering the principles of aiming. This subject is often dealt with only briefly, and consequently many beginners are unable to understand fully the principles involved, with the result that they experience disappointment in their early efforts to hit the target without sufficient knowledge to correct what may be a simple error. This can lead to a dwindling interest in the sport and the possibility of lost membership.

It is all very well for a beginner, in the early stages of archery, to be told that it matters little whether the target be hit or not; this may well be so – in fact emphasis on correct stance, bow position, draw technique and loose is of primary importance in the early days – but there is no doubt of the value of the satisfaction of hitting a target, even at a very short range. Therefore, it is quite important that early lessons in theory should be devoted to aiming.

THE THEORY OF AIMING

Generally speaking, except for a very short distance, an arrow does not travel in a straight line. As it loses speed, it starts to fall in a low curve. This part of the arrow's flight is called the Trajectory. If this is viewed from above, the path the arrow takes is the Line of Flight, and this can be deflected from a straight line by wind variations. The course of the arrow has initially to be calculated so that it homes on the target. This initial calculation is the result of trial and error, and is based on the fact that there are several constant factors by means of which the pattern of aiming is constructed. They comprise: the eye of the archer (A), the target or aiming mark (B), and the sighting device (C). These, combined with the Angle of Elevation and the Line of Direction of the arrow (a continuation of the Preparation Line) pivoted from a constant anchor point location, provide a reasonably accurate method of aiming a bow.

52

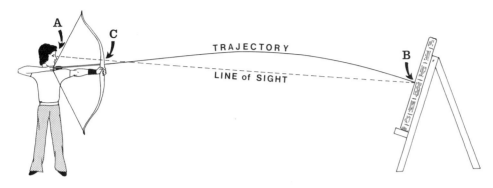

The principles of aiming.

PRACTICAL AIMING

For a moment let us assume that there is no sighting device with the bow; then the ideal aiming arrangement occurs when the Line of Flight cuts the Trajectory of the arrow exactly at the pile of the arrow at full draw. The arrow pile can then be visually placed on the gold, which will be hit by the released arrow. Let us assume that this aim is taken and the arrow overshoots the target. Some adjustment has then to be made. It is clear that the elevation of the arrow has to be depressed to enable the lesser distance to be reached. With all other positions remaining constant, this will result in the view of the target appearing higher in relation to the arrow. If we now use the sighting device, adjusted to appear on the gold, it will be seen that this aiming position can be accurately assumed time after time. This device performs the same function as a foresight on a rifle, but, unlike that weapon, a bow has no backsight. It is, therefore, important to remember that the Angle of Elevation of the arrow should be accurately controlled; any slight variation at one end or the other produces an enlarged error at the target.

The method of adjusting the elevation of the arrow is by slightly moving the body from the waist, without moving the hips or legs. Do not move the bow arm up or down from the shoulders as this destroys the continuity of line of the shaft arm and arrow, and spoils the relation of all other positions which you have so carefully perfected beforehand.

Set positions of the sighting pin for different distances can be established by means of an adjustable slide on the sight, but they may vary slightly according to the weather conditions. For example, a following wind blowing down the range towards the targets can lift the arrow in flight and extend its range, so the sight will be set a little higher than normal. Alternatively, a head wind from the targets will tend to depress and shorten the flight of the arrow, necessitating the use of a lower sighting mark. Cross-winds will affect the Line of Flight, and these have to be allowed for by lateral adjustments or aiming off into the wind, and can only be judged by experience and common sense.

By an intelligent application of the theory of aiming and by carefully putting into practice the principles explained, a more consistent pattern of shooting will become easier to achieve.

The archer's view of the ideal aiming arrangement with the pile of the arrow on the gold.

Aiming with a sighting device, in this case a ring sight, which is adjustable vertically and horizontally.

A simple sight with a sliding head. This can easily be mounted on the back of a bow.

Right: Adjusting a sight. This shows the general arrangement by which a bow-sight is mounted on the back of a bow. A scale is calibrated with various distances according to individual preference.

Loosing

The loose is the most critical of all the points of archery, and extra effort in the management of finger movements in the early days will prove beneficial as you become more skilled. Whereas with some application a novice can soon manage this action, the perfecting of a correct loosing movement is not easy to acquire and takes considerable practice. The action required is simple. Once the arrow, bow, and string are positioned at full draw in exactly the right alignment towards the mark, all the stored energy must be suddenly released so that the bow can propel the arrow to its required destination. This works extremely well – if none of the positioning is disturbed.

A GOOD LOOSE

Let us examine the moment before the loose. The string is held back by half-bent fingers in an unnatural tension, the bow is held forward in space to just the right distance, and the eye is momentarily mesmerized by a good aim on the target. Alter one of these factors by a fraction and the shot is spoiled. There are many other considerations too which, once settled, must not be altered. Imagine that the archer stands firm and then, suddenly, his fingers holding the string are not there; and you have a reasonably good idea of the sought-after action of loosing. The string must not slip gradually off the fingers, neither must they be snatched off the string; the loose must be smooth and easy, without any jerk.

The recommended method of achieving a good loose consists of a series of carefully controlled simultaneous movements. The shaft arm, holding back the arrow, should be relaxed and held in position by the back muscles. If a little extra muscular effort is exerted from the back this will result in the arm being moved slightly back, in the direction of the Draw Force Line. This results in the string being pressed back a little harder on to the chin. At the same moment the fingers holding the string should be straightened, and the arrow leaves the bow.

These movements, which are hardly perceptible to the observer, must be exactly co-ordinated. If all this occurs correctly, no change in string position results up to its final release, and the loose is clean and sharp.

The fingers should be relaxed and not stiff or taut when they are straightened, and it is most important that all three fingers should quit the string simultaneously.

Because of the released tension of the drawn bow, the drawing hand will continue to move backwards, close to the neck. Often this backward movement is continued for an inch or so, or even further, but provided a clean loose is achieved there is no harm in this. However, it is important to keep the hand from turning until after the loose has been completed. Wrist and hand are relaxed, and this relaxation will be apparent once the string is free of the fingers.

Ready for the loose. The lack of tension shown in this study reflects the calm and methodical approach which prepares the way for better archery.

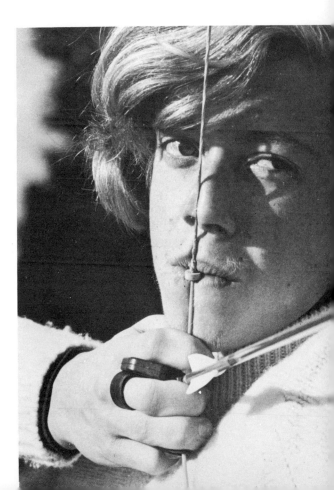

In this action shot the archer has released his fingers unequally, tensed his hand, and dropped the elbow of his drawing arm.

An example of how the drawing hand can be turned a full 90° on release, a natural motion which should be controlled.

Right: The Follow Through in which the bow arm and hand have travelled back in line, close to the neck; wrist and hand are relaxed and straight; and the bow has remained steady until the arrow has reached its mark.

The tendency to allow the arrow to creep forward momentarily before the loose must be carefully controlled. Remember that the arrow must remain exactly at the same drawn length until the actual moment of release. A popular gadget to provide an audible signal of the correct drawn length is now commonly used. This is the 'clicker', a light spring under which the arrow is drawn, and when the exact distance is reached it snaps back with a click. At this moment the arrow should be released, which involves careful timing of the aim and the final extra pressure of the loosing process. The use of such a device is a matter of personal choice, but it is far better to perfect a satisfactory loose without such aids.

BLIND LOOSING

A method which has proved useful in practising the loose is what is called 'blind loosing'. Stand close to a target, say two yards or so away, and with your eyes closed go through the whole sequence of drawing and loosing. Without any outside distractions you can concentrate more deeply on all the things that should be done, and a good clean loose will soon be recognized through the feel of the action. This also eliminates the additional mental and physical activities needed for aiming, and you can, therefore, concentrate on the all-important moment of loose. If you do decide to indulge in blind loosing, remember two things: the eyes should be closed for a period of time, not just for a moment while the action takes place, and above all ask a friend to supervise this activity from the aspect of safety.

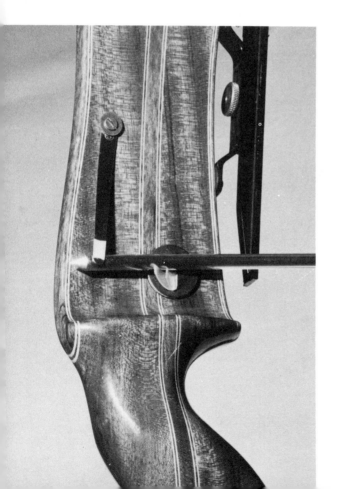

Two useful accessories: the 'clicker' with an arrow being drawn back under it, and an arrow rest designed to minimize friction when the arrow is released.

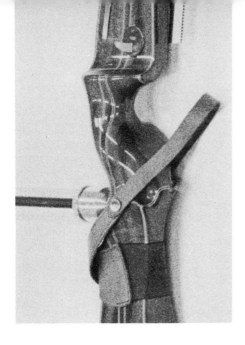

By slipping his hand through this bow sling an archer with a loose grip prevents the bow jumping from his hand on release.

THE FOLLOW THROUGH

When the arrow is loosed, the released tension tends to allow both arms and bow to change their positions. The bow hand and arm should remain exactly in the position they were in the aim, and the shaft arm and hand should move back in the direction of the Draw Force Line.

Some archers use a very light grip on the bow, and to prevent it from springing from the hand they use some form of simple harness. There is no harm in letting the bow move freely at this stage, so long as the released string does not strike the bracer or arm. Remain perfectly still, with hands, arms and body in just the same position as when the loose was performed, until the arrow has found its mark. Under no circumstances must you watch the flight of the arrow, and your visual aim on the target must be maintained. This passive part of the shooting sequence is known as the Follow Through. Lack of control at this stage can cause trouble. If, for example, your hands fall away before the arrow reaches the target, there is a tendency for them to start moving at, or even before, the moment of loosing. The practice of a Follow Through for each arrow ensures that the complete rhythm of shooting is not disturbed or abruptly curtailed. It is after this that you can relax, consider the success or otherwise of your shot, mentally correct any errors, clear your mind and prepare for the next arrow.

A good Follow Through; hand and arm in line, fingers relaxed and body position maintained. In this example the archer's loose grip has allowed the bow to swing. Note the use of the bow sling.

Faults and Their Correction

Once the whole sequence of shooting one arrow is mastered, it is then necessary to do everything in exactly the same way for each subsequent shot. This need for consistency in every movement is something which we have repeated more than once, but it can only be achieved by consciously thinking through the sequence of shooting each individual arrow. It is true that after considerable practice the thought processes become almost automatic. When this stage is reached, it is well to remember that not only must you think of what you are doing but you must also consider whether what you are doing is right! Combined with this mental process, you have to monitor constantly your performance in so far as the end result is concerned. In other words, the destination of each arrow must be considered in relation to the previous one. Thus the combination of 'What did I do?' and 'Did I do it correctly?', together with a mental record of where the arrow finished, will form an analysis of your own shooting technique and performance, and a basis for correction if necessary – or a signal to repeat the sequence exactly, if everything was as it should be.

TYPES OF FAULTS

The correction of faults in archery is a constant process, and this applies equally to beginners and to the most skilled archers. Even Olympic and World Champions have never been able to hit the target in exactly the same spot with every arrow for the duration of a round, so, if we discount adverse weather conditions, there must be at least one other factor which disturbs the perfect sequence. In general the majority of faults can be attributed to bad individual technique. Amongst such faults may be those that are essentially physical (wrong body, arm and hand positions, incorrect movements and so on), some which relate to timing, and others which are mental. Outside distractions such as fatigue, or even anger and frustration, are other causes which result in bad shooting, but it can be argued that such matters encourage bad technique, which in turn spoils an otherwise good shot. Other causes of incorrect shooting can be identified as technical faults, in other words those which include faulty or incorrect equipment.

THE RIGHT MENTAL ATTITUDE

Let us first consider the archer's mental attitude. Undoubtedly the mood of the archer has a general effect on his shooting and, as everyone is apt to feel 'up' at some times and 'down' at others, we can begin to understand one of the reasons why a good day's shooting can be followed by a bad day. If it were possible to cultivate an 'archery mood' in preparation for shooting, how much easier it would be to maintain a steady, if not brilliant, performance! It is rare for a human being to be able to turn on a critical mental power, but to be able to give complete attention to your own personal rhythm of shooting, without being distracted in any way, is a habit not too difficult to acquire, and once it has been learnt it is easy to maintain. It clears the way for good shooting and ultimate personal satisfaction.

It is easy to be told not to do this or that and quite simple to correct faults if they are of a practical nature. It is also just as easy to be told to avoid a certain emotion, but extremely difficult to quell a feeling of momentary anger, frustration or disappointment. If you take time to think out the problems that you may encounter, and endeavour quietly and deliberately to settle each one in turn, this will help create the best mental attitude to archery. Strive always to improve your own personal performance and be confident in your own ability to improve.

BASIC FAULTS

An excellent training film* begins with the words: 'Almost the whole of what the technique of target archery is about is contained in the proper shooting of one arrow into a target.' Let us examine some of the most common faults which can spoil that 'proper shooting'. The four basic results of inaccurate shooting are:

---

* *Target Archery*, Part 1: *Groundwork*, and Part 2: *Shooting*, Gerard Holdsworth Productions Ltd.

64

1. Shooting high on the target or over.
2. Shooting low on the target or short.
3. Shooting to the right or missing right.
4. Shooting to the left or missing left.

The following permutations can be added to the above; high-right, low-right, low-left, and high-left.

These are consistent errors, which usually result from bad technique and sometimes through a combination of several faults, each of which must be found and corrected. It is easier to pinpoint a fault if at least six arrows are considered; it is of little use to isolate the performance of one arrow. The better the arrows are grouped on the target, the easier it is to correct their collective position, and this applies to a large extent if the arrows are in a good group in the ground.

A typical 'scatter' where arrows have struck haphazardly on the target and in the ground, which indicates that a number of faults may be present.

Vertical errors, shooting high.

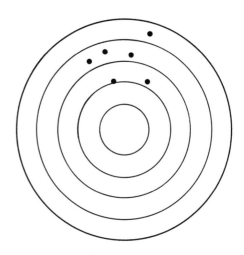

VERTICAL ERRORS

Let us first discuss the causes of vertical errors which are entirely due to faulty equipment. Several minor mishaps can produce shooting errors such as the sight slipping up or down the track; bent arrows; slight expansion or stretching of the string, which can let the bow down; alteration of the bracing height; or the centre serving on the string may have slipped, changing the position of the nocking point. Several other matters of this nature can occur and the cure is obvious – make sure that your equipment is in good order every time you use it, and throughout shooting carry out periodic checks to see that all these items are as they should be.

Shooting high

This can result from over-drawing, which in turn may be due to an incorrect stance. Associated with this is the over-drawing which results from using arrows which are too long, or re-locating the anchor-point further back along the jaw, thus drawing the arrow back too far.

The arrow must remain steady in line, and any movement which pushes the forward end up or the rear end down produces a high shot. For example, dropping the shaft hand can cause this or opening the mouth has the same effect. Pinching the arrow can also lift it off the arrow rest, or the arrow can be put off line by raising the bow hand.

66

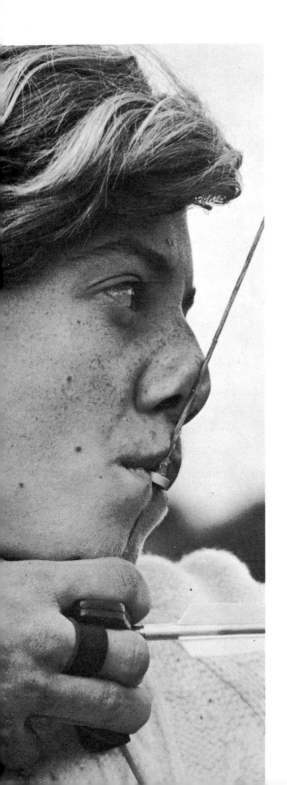

There should be no space between fingers and chin, and some archers find the use of a 'kisser' helpful in consistently finding the right location. The kisser shown here consists of a small rubber disc, which must not exceed 1cm. in width, fastened to the string.

If the bow is tilted backwards, possibly caused by exerting undue pressure below the centre of the pressure point of the hand on the bow, or 'heeling', a high shot will result. Additional faults in this example include bending the body backwards, turning up the bow hand and not opening the fingers cleanly on release.

The moment of release is all-important and a bad loose can produce any amount of errors. A sharpened loose, or a snatched loose performed in an inconsistent manner, usually sends an arrow flying higher than intended. Care must be taken to release the string with all your fingers at the same time. If the loose is achieved by letting the fingers lag behind each other, the arrow will not fly as it should. If the third finger looses first, the arrow will fly higher.

Improper control of the bow can produce inaccurate shooting. A high shot will result if the bow is pushed forward at the moment of loosing.

Vertical errors, shooting low.

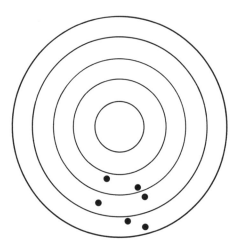

Shooting low

Many of the faults which produce low flying arrows are the opposite of those which cause high shots. A very common cause is under-drawing, which can be the result of several things such as 'creeping' or allowing the arrow to move forward before the loose. This causes loss of power in the bow and prevents the 'spine' of the arrow from reacting properly. The re-location of the anchor-point forward, thus producing an under-drawn arrow, is another matter which must be avoided. Allowing the arrow to creep forward can also be caused by a bow arm which imperceptibly sags or collapses from holding the aim too long.

Control of the bow is again important if low arrows are to be avoided.

The loose can contribute to low arrows in the opposite way to that which we described as producing high shots. If the forefinger is allowed to loose the string first, arrows will fly low.

In this action shot the young archer has spoiled his shot by dropping his bow hand on release, a common cause of low flying arrows, which in turn may be due to the drawing elbow being held too high.

If excess pressure is applied above the centre of the pressure point of the hand on the bow, called 'topping', then low shots will result.

HORIZONTAL ERRORS

Shooting left

The proper handling and control of the bow is important if these errors are to be avoided. First, make sure that the bow is not low-strung, i.e. check that the bracing height is correct. There will be a tendency for arrows to fly to the left if the bow is held too tightly and if it is turned to the right in the hand. This is described as 'applying excessive torque'.

The string position must be controlled; it must always be released in the true Line of Flight. Discrepancies here can be the result of jerking the shaft hand away from the face on release (remember it must travel back in line, close to the neck), or re-location of the anchor-point too far to the right. Another matter to watch is keeping the string hand vertical; if it is tilted out of true, it has the effect of producing a kink in the string or a 'dog-leg', thus disturbing the true line of the string on release.

Right: If the bow is tilted to the right (as the archer sees it), arrows will fly to the left. Another cause of this error can be jerking the shaft hand away from the face on release.

Horizontal errors, shooting left.

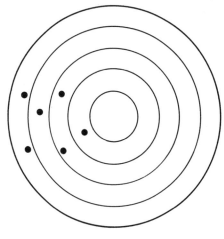

70

Interruption of the path of the released string can also produce the same bad fault, throwing it off line, and this can occur if it hits the bracer or fouls loose clothing.

Arrows which are allowed to creep will also tend to fly left, as well as low.

Shooting right

The last of the common errors in shooting can be caused by the opposite of some of the faults which produced horizontal errors to the left. The handling and control of the bow is again important: a slackened grip or the application of torque in the opposite direction can cause arrows to fly to the right.

A bad loose such as not opening the fingers cleanly on release can also contribute to this error. Additionally, make sure that the string is not held too deeply on the fingers.

Left: Tilting the bow to the left (as the archer sees it), is a frequent cause of arrows flying to the right. Note also the bad after-loose position of the shaft hand, and the fact that the archer is leaning backwards.

Horizontal errors, shooting right.

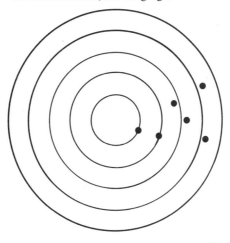

71

The above series of faults in technique is by no means complete; what we have outlined are those which most generally appear. If the proper technique is not applied consistently, one or more of these faults can creep in and each time this happens you must make the corrections immediately. Some of these faults are easy to rectify, others take a little more time, particularly if they have become a habit.

It must be emphasised that many archers make good scores by evolving their own minor points of technique; this is not a bad thing, provided that everything is consistently performed. However, the routines which we have explained, if carried out diligently, can improve your shooting, but this must be accompanied by regular practice and a desire to better your previous performance. There is a great personal satisfaction in discovering that you can do better, but like all discoveries it is the result of a certain amount of perseverance. The more you persevere, the more you will improve; the more you improve, the greater your enjoyment in shooting a bow.

Safety and Etiquette

Let it be said at the outset that *a bow is a lethal weapon and under no circumstances must it be considered as a toy*. Properly handled, it can provide the means of giving you many years of enjoyment; careless use can result in accidents and even loss of life. Accordingly, an intelligent observance of some simple safety rules is essential; most of these rules are common sense. However, it is worth repeating those matters which must be observed when practising archery and which are long-established regulations observed by every archery club and association where organized shooting takes place.

THE ARCHERY FIELD

Shooting should only take place at an archery field officially recognised as such. The indiscriminate use of gardens, parks, common land or public places, no matter how safe they may appear, is contrary to the current official rules, and any archery practice which takes place under such arrangements would not be recognised, either for insurance purposes or in connection with the recording of scores under the various schemes approved by the Grand National Archery Society.

A line of targets prepared for a major tournament, in this case the Grand National Archery Meeting. They are numbered or lettered from left to right and each alternate target has a black spot to assist identification from the shooting line.

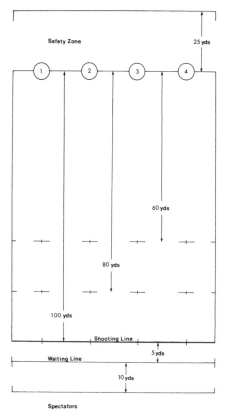

Safety Zone

25 yds

60 yds

80 yds

100 yds

Shooting Line

5 yds

Waiting Line

10 yds

Spectators

A typical lay-out of an archery field for a York round. The measurements would be in Metric when shooting under International Rules takes place. Normally the shooting line is moved forward to adjust to the different distances of a round, and the targets remain static. To take advantage of the best daylight conditions the ideal orientation in the Northern hemisphere is roughly North/South, with the archers shooting towards the North.

By being a member of a properly constituted club which is affiliated to the national body for archery (the G.N.A.S. in the case of the United Kingdom and the equivalent national associations in nearly sixty other countries), an archer can take part in organized competitions con-' trolled by a series of rules which have been carefully evolved with the interests of the individual in mind. In the case of the G.N.A.S. the benefits of affiliation include, amongst other things, automatic participation in a Public Liability Insurance scheme. Briefly, this allows insurance cover for associated clubs and their members in respect of injury or damage caused in the course of the sport, but only when the shooting is under the auspices of the G.N.A.S. or an affiliated body. Therefore practice which is not organized by a club, say in an archer's own garden, is not covered by the scheme.

SAFETY RULES

A general rule which, although brief, deals completely with the way in which a bow should be handled is contained in G.N.A.S. *Rules of Shooting*. It reads: 'A bow may not be drawn except on the shooting line and in the direction of the targets' (Rule 104 [p]). Each archer must have complete mastery over every shot. To aim indiscriminately, without knowing where the arrow will land, is thoughtless and an unforgivable practice. The unpredictability of an arrow shot straight into the air or the danger of a shaft shot so that it goes out of sight, over an obstacle or into bushes for example, illustrates the type of uncontrolled shooting to be avoided. In any case, there is very little satisfaction in undisciplined archery as, after all, the whole idea is to hit the target!

It is important to exercise complete control over the movements of everyone on the archery field, no matter whether they are taking part in the shooting or are there as spectators or visitors, and the rules are quite clear on this point. All those participating move to the shooting line on a signal given by whoever is in charge of shooting, normally a Judge or Field Captain (Rule 104[d]). Each archer shoots three arrows and then retires until all the other archers shooting at the same target have also shot three. The process is repeated until all archers

The move forward to the targets after the completion of each end, with a watchful eye for arrows which have fallen short. Bows are left behind the shooting line.

This clearly shows the five-yard gap between shooters and archers waiting their turn to shoot.

75

have shot six arrows – this is known as an 'end' (Rule 103[c]). The Judge signals the completion of each end and the archers then advance to the targets to take scores (Rule 104[d]). Unless archers are actually shooting or they are moving to and from the shooting line, they must remain behind the waiting line (Rule 104[q]).

There is a warning cry which should be used by any archer if he sees some good reason why shooting should stop, and this shout of 'Fast!' is immediately recognised and obeyed. Alternatively several blasts on a whistle are the recognised danger signal. This can indicate some form of danger such as unauthorised persons getting perilously near the danger area, an unsafe target, or an arrow hanging from the target instead of sticking into it which could be damaged by further shots.

The best way to withdraw arrows from a target, which prevents the shafts being bent and also protects the target face from being damaged by torn or enlarged arrow holes.

A 'hanger' which could be damaged by other arrows or deflect and spoil subsequent shots. Shooting will stop until this arrow is replaced by a Judge.

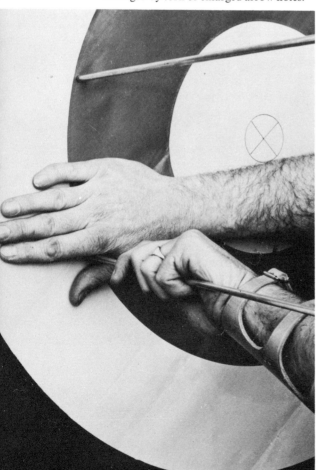

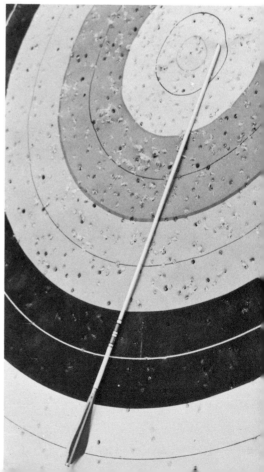

RETRIEVING ARROWS

The advance from the shooting line to the targets in order to take scores is an orderly procedure, but be on the alert for arrows which have fallen short. These should be collected during the move forward, and care must be taken when they are drawn from the ground. Pull them straight back, making sure that your feet or another person's are not in the way. If you pull an arrow out of the ground clumsily, you may well bend it. Sometimes an arrow will hide itself quite flat in the grass; then to save damaging fletchings, it is best to retrieve it by pulling it through the grass in line with its flight. These hints are just as much to protect your equipment as to protect feet and legs from a nasty jab by a hastily uprooted arrow. Similar care must be observed when drawing arrows from a target; see that no-one stands in the way, and pull the arrows out in exactly the opposite direction to which they entered.

Use your tassel to wipe each arrow, particularly if it has been in the ground, inspect it to see that the fletchings are intact, and make sure that it has not been bent or dented.

UNWRITTEN RULES

It is only courteous to show consideration towards other archers who are striving just as hard as you are to improve. It is discourteous for any archer on the shooting line or elsewhere on the field to talk in a loud voice to the annoyance of others. It can be quite distracting to a person concentrating on shooting, particularly at the critical moment just before the loose, to be disturbed by a sudden noise of any kind, and a thoughtless exclamation can, and often does, ruin what otherwise would have been a good shot. It is bad sportsmanship to talk to another competitor who obviously prefers to remain silent.

It is considered to be very bad manners to walk up and down the shooting line studying and comparing other archers' scores.

Some archers pay considerable sums of money for their tackle, others provide for themselves very economically, but, whatever their value, these possessions are highly prized by their owners and a good archer cares for his equipment like a mother for her child. It is extremely bad manners to touch another's equipment without first seeking the owner's permission. Accidents can happen, however, and, if an archer breaks another's arrow, for instance, through his own carelessness, he pays for it on the spot.

TAKING SCORES

The order in which archers shoot at their respective targets is shown on a Target List for each target. Normally No. 3 on that list becomes Target Captain and No. 4 the Lieutenant. The Captain is responsible for the orderly conduct of shooting on his particular target, and it is he who is also responsible for seeing that the scores are correctly recorded, which are counter-checked by the Lieutenant (Rules 103[b] [i] and 105[b]). Not all archers welcome this job, as it involves extra responsibility in addition to one's own shooting. However, it has to be done and it is up to all the other archers on the target to make the task as easy as possible. Calling the scores in a uniform manner, for example, avoids confusion and it is customary to call scores in groups of three, e.g. '7–7–5', pause '5–5–3', highest scores first. Do not go behind the target to retrieve arrows until your score has been recorded. At the end of a round, do not forget to thank the Target Captain for the work he has done on your behalf.

Left: Note the Target Captain, with score board, ready to take down the scores. No arrows are withdrawn until all scores have been called and recorded.

Top right: Each arrow is identified by its owner and its value called in sequence. To touch an arrow, or the target face, before it is scored means its disqualification.

Far right: After scores have been recorded, arrows which have missed and finish 'in the green' are identified and collected by their owners.

Right: A general purpose score sheet which is so arranged that each dozen and each distance is separately totalled. In addition to the score the number of hits and golds is important as some awards are based on these additional factors.

ARCHERY SCORE SHEET									
YARDS							HITS	SCORE	GOLDS
1									
2									
3									
4									
5									
6									
					TOTAL YARDS				
YARDS									
1									
2									
3									
4									
					TOTAL YARDS				
YARDS									
1									
2									
3									
SCORER		TOTAL YARDS							
		TOTAL YARDS							
CHECKED BY		TOTAL YARDS							
		GRAND TOTAL							

An arrow touching two colours, such as the one shown here, scores the higher value. Any doubtful arrows or differences of opinion as to their value are resolved by the Judge.

These targets are securely lashed down to prevent them from being blown over. The exact height and angle of the targets is laid down in G.N.A.S. *Rules*.

Those who are responsible for such matters as ground lay-out and club equipment invariably ensure that targets are securely anchored to prevent them from toppling over in a sudden gust of wind; in fact this is a compulsory precaution (Rule 101[c]). A target full of arrows which has been blown over is a sorry sight; it is good sense to make sure that the target you are shooting at has been firmly tied down.

Incorrect handling of target bosses can quickly loosen the cords that bind the straw together and the boss becomes flabby, weak and misshapen. Always carry a boss, never roll it along the ground and always store it flat, not on edge.

Help to maintain a neat and orderly area behind the waiting line. Nowadays archers attend shoots with much more equipment, both for shooting and for their own personal comfort, than a few years ago. The scene behind the line at any moderate sized tournament takes on the appearance of a temporary encampment, with large gaily coloured umbrellas, tents and every sort of portable comfort that can be imagined. Do make a special effort to keep your equipment and paraphernalia neat and tidy, use the ground quiver for bows and arrows not in immediate use, make sure that other archers have clear access to the shooting line, and please do not leave litter.

80

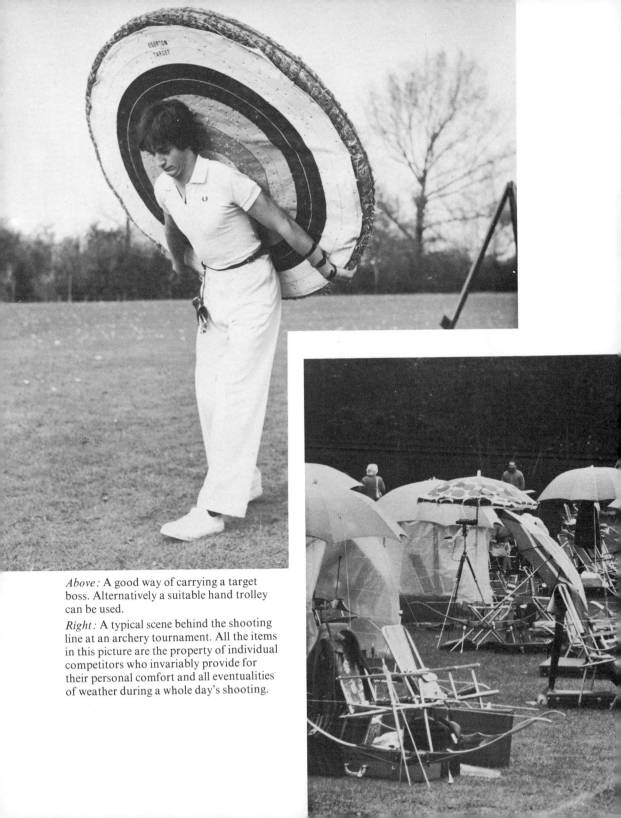

Above: A good way of carrying a target boss. Alternatively a suitable hand trolley can be used.

Right: A typical scene behind the shooting line at an archery tournament. All the items in this picture are the property of individual competitors who invariably provide for their personal comfort and all eventualities of weather during a whole day's shooting.

Competitive Archery

TARGET ARCHERY

There are a number of different forms of archery which are regularly practised today, the most popular being Target Archery. This consists of shooting a specified number of arrows at targets of standard sizes at pre-determined distances. 'Rounds' vary according to the standard of proficiency, and the age and sex of the archer. The rounds officially recognised by the G.N.A.S. and which are used in competitive shooting by clubs and societies affiliated to that body are listed in Appendix A (Rules 106[a], 300, and 501[a]). They include a special series devised for junior archers (up to 18 years of age). In the Metric Rounds the two longer distances are shot on a 122 cm ten-zone target face, and the two shorter distances on a 80 cm ten-zone target face under F.I.T.A. rules (Fédération Internationale de Tir à l'Arc). In all other rounds, unless specified otherwise, the standard British 122 cm five-zone target face is used. In every round the longer or longest distance is shot first, and the shorter or shortest distance last.

It is good sense to start shooting complete rounds early in your archery career and, once you have reached a reasonable proficiency in the shorter and less arduous rounds, you should progress steadily to the rounds which are recognised for competition purposes in your particular class. For example, the Bristol series of rounds are those used for the Junior National Championship as follows:

Bristol I   for boys under 18 years of age.
Bristol II   for boys under 16, and girls under 18 years of age.
Bristol III for boys under 14, and girls under 16 years of age.
Bristol IV for boys under 12, and girls under 13 years of age.

An archer may enter for a round in a higher age group than his or her own, but not for a round in a lower age group. The Bristol Rounds, particularly those with the longer distances, can be compared to senior rounds in terms of duration and distance. Do not be too ambitious to begin with; it is far better to progress gradually to the longer distances.

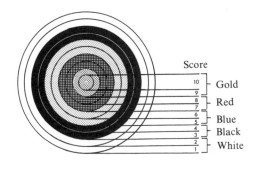

	Score	
	10	Gold
	9	
	8	Red
	7	
	6	Blue
	5	
	4	Black
	3	
	2	White
	1	

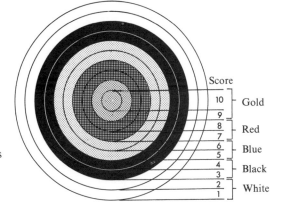

International target faces showing colours and scoring values: (*top*) 80cm ten-zone face; (*bottom*) 122cm ten-zone face.

	Score	
	10	Gold
	9	
	8	Red
	7	
	6	Blue
	5	
	4	Black
	3	
	2	White
	1	

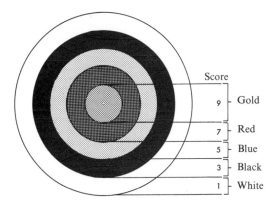

Standard British 122cm five-zone target face showing colours and scoring values.

	Score	
	9	Gold
	7	Red
	5	Blue
	3	Black
	1	White

83

TOURNAMENTS

Organized competitions are arranged at club, county, regional and national levels, and there are ample opportunities to enter tournaments when your standard has reached a certain level. Apart from selection, when certain archers are chosen to represent their club, county or other organization because of their consistently high performance, there are numerous tournaments which are open to all archers whatever their standard. It is a good idea to participate in competitions for several reasons. Firstly, it is helpful to have the opportunity to meet other archers, to discuss and compare your own progress with others of similar standards, and to make new friends who have the same enthusiasm for archery. Secondly, there are benefits to be gained from the wider experience offered by these gatherings in shooting under competitive conditions, from which you should gain confidence in your own shooting ability. Lastly, the prospect of entering a tournament encourages archers to do their best and, what is more important, to put in that extra practice beforehand. It is rewarding to see your name on the results list progressing to higher positions, and a great satisfaction to see that you have done better at each subsequent tournament.

SCHOOLS ARCHERY

Schools have long recognised the importance of organized games and sports, and archery is frequently included in the curriculum. The Association for Archery in Schools, formed in 1963, is a body which attends to the needs of young archers by the general promotion of the sport, arranging tournaments and other competitive shooting, activities which might possibly have been neglected by organizations mainly devoted to adult archery. The A.A.S. runs a Summer Postal League, which is open to teams of four juniors, and an Inter-Schools Team Tournament held annually at the end of the season. Both these events are well supported and indicate the enthusiasm and interest shown by budding world champions. In addition this Association has recently introduced the Archery Achievement Scheme, open to juniors not only within this Association but also to those who are members of properly affiliated archery clubs generally. Juniors who reach certain standards can qualify for badge awards, which indicate their progress in the sport. Many clubs apart from school

84

archery clubs have active junior sections and every encouragement is given to young archers to become full participating members of such clubs.

Perhaps you may decide to enter the Duke of Edinburgh's Award Scheme for boys and girls, which includes archery as a 'pursuit' for boys and an 'interest' for girls. For a candidate to qualify he or she has to satisfy examiners as to his or her aptitude and enthusiasm in accordance with an official syllabus which is far from arduous or difficult. A candidate needs to be an enthusiastic archer and a trier, but not necessarily a good shot. Through this scheme, which is designed to help young people to be good citizens, many youngsters not only learn the art of archery but in addition learn how to be good club members.

Concentration on doing well at a schools archery tournament. The two archers at the end of the shooting line are left-handed.

VARIETY IN ARCHERY

Throughout this book we have concentrated particularly on Target Archery, but there are a number of other forms of archery which can be pursued, which offer variety in the sport. However, it must be emphasized that in some of these variants special shooting techniques are required, therefore it is far better to perfect your Target Shooting techniques before experimenting with other forms of shooting.

The different forms of shooting which are covered by the G.N.A.S. *Rules of Shooting* are as follows:

Field Archery

This consists of shooting at special targets, either bold black and white circles, or animal figures with scoring areas superimposed upon them, placed at a great variety of marked or unmarked distances in rough country. Some classes of Field Archery forbid any form of aiming device, which requires the employment of special techniques known as instinctive shooting.

Left: Flight Archery is a highly specialized form of shooting with the sole object of reaching the greatest distance. There are three classes of competition; for standard target bows, for flight bows, which are specially made for this form of archery, and a free-style class in which any type of bow, other than cross-bows, can be used. A special technique of shooting is employed which is designed to get the greatest amount of 'cast' from a bow to project the arrow as far as possible.

Right: Popinjay Shooting requires a mast ninety feet high, on the top of which is a series of 'birds' on a framework of perches. The birds are made of wood and decorated with tufts of coloured feathers, and each has a scoring value which is awarded as it is dislodged. Archers shoot in turn almost vertically with blunt-headed arrows for which a special stance is required.

Indoor Archery has become popular in recent years as a means of continuing Target Archery throughout the winter months when weather conditions are not suitable for shooting out-of-doors. Special rounds have been devised for Indoor Archery and they are listed in Appendix A.

Clout Shooting

An ancient form of archery, which still survives, where the target is marked out on the ground and is shot at from much greater distances than in Target Archery – 9 score yards for gentlemen and 7 score yards for ladies – 180 and 140 yards respectively. Normal target equipment is used, but to reach these distances it is often necessary to shoot high into the air to drop the arrows down on to the target.

Archery Golf

A novel form of archery in which a bow and arrows are substituted for a golf club and balls. It can only be played on a regular golf course, and the idea is to duplicate each of the golfer's shots by comparable archery shots. A flight shot replaces the tee shot of the golfer, the golfer's approach shot is matched by a regular target shot from a bow, and lastly the putt is duplicated when the archer holes out by shooting at a white disc of card in the green.

Administration

The *Constitution* of the G.N.A.S. declares that the objects of the Society are 'the promotion and encouragement of archery in all its forms, other than Bow Hunting'. In chapter 8 we mentioned the Public Liability Insurance scheme administered by G.N.A.S., and in this section we have grouped together most of the principal ways in which the G.N.A.S. fulfils its objectives. They fall under two main headings – official rules and other matters which are desirable but not compulsory.

The Grand National Archery Society is the governing body for archery throughout the United Kingdom and similar national associations exist in many other countries. All are affiliated to the Fédération Internationale de Tir à l'Arc (F.I.T.A.), which is the overall governing body for the sport. Members of archery clubs affiliated to the G.N.A.S., which includes clubs situated within the British Commonwealth and Empire, must strictly adhere to the shooting regulations whenever shooting takes place. These regulations are published as *Rules of Shooting*, and must be carefully studied for each particular form of archery practised. They are too lengthy to be repeated in full in these pages, although we have already quoted several pertinent extracts from these regulations in the foregoing chapters, plus the fact that from time to time they are amended. You should, therefore, always make sure that your personal copy of the *Rules is* brought

The badge adopted by the Grand National Archery Society. The motto of the Society is: *Stout arm, Strong bow and Steady eye; Union, True heart and Courtesy.*

up to date. The shooting regulations are designed for your safety and the safety of others, and they have been devised after many years of practical experience with the overall object of making archery more enjoyable by the application of simple, common sense procedures.

We have previously mentioned international (F.I.T.A.) rules for Target Archery; these are contained in *Constitutions and Rules*, published by that body. However, an interpretation of the F.I.T.A. *Rules* which most generally apply have been included in G.N.A.S. *Rules of Shooting*.

CLASSIFICATION SCHEME

In the Classification Scheme (Parts VII and VIII of G.N.A.S. *Rules*) certain titles are awarded to archers according to their level of performance. The qualifications become progressively more difficult, until the exalted rank of Grand Master Bowman is reached. Though few archers reach this exacting standard, there is ample scope in the lesser ranks of Master Bowman, and Class I, II and III Archers. The scheme is operated quite simply. To gain Class I, II or III an archer must shoot, during the calendar year, three rounds of, or better than, the scores set out in a table in the *Rules*. These rounds must be shot at a Club Target Day (Rule 150), or at a meeting organized by the G.N.A.S., when a minimum of two archers are shooting together. Immediately the requisite scores are made, the upgrading occurs, but, if during a second year the archer is unable to make the necessary scores in his class, then he is relegated to a class below.

The titles of Grand Master Bowman and Master Bowman are treated specially. The standard of the former has been made very high indeed and qualifications can only be gained at major tournaments, whereas, although the standard of Master Bowman is high, only half the qualifying rounds have to be shot at major meetings.

Juniors can qualify for the title of Master Bowman, and for Class I, II and III Archers. To qualify as Master Bowman a junior must shoot four of the following rounds (Rule 504):

Boys: York/Bristol I, Men's FITA/Ladies FITA (Metric I).

Girls: Hereford/Bristol II, Ladies FITA (Metric I)/Metric II.

These rounds must include at least one, with a maximum of three, Metric/FITA rounds, three of which may be shot at a Club Target Day, supervised by a senior, and one at least must be shot at a major tournament. To achieve the title

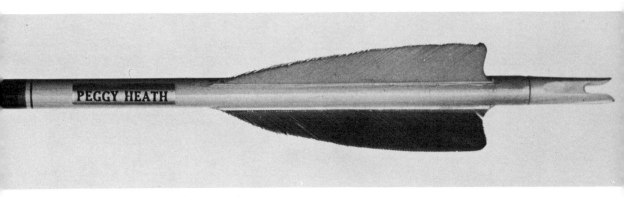

rows must be marked with the archer's name or initials.

le 103(e) states that 'An arrow shall be deemed not to have been shot, if the archer can touch ith his bow without moving his feet from their position in relation to the shooting line. In ch case another arrow may be shot in its place.'

When six consecutive arrows are shot into the gold, it is known as a 'perfect end'. Six Gold badges are awarded for this achievement. Juniors can qualify as this 14-year-old has proved.

of Class I, II or III Archer a junior must shoot special qualifying scores under the same arrangements as those which apply to senior archers. The actual scores required are published in the G.N.A.S. *Rules of Shooting* and, as these are changed from time to time, you should refer to your up-to-date Rules 504 and 505.

THE HANDICAP SCHEME

This scheme (Part IX of G.N.A.S. *Rules*), like the Classification Scheme, is operated by individual clubs and a set of Handicap Tables is issued by the G.N.A.S. which includes precise instructions for its operation. A special set of tables is provided for juniors. The principle by which the scheme works is that the score for any given round has a corresponding handicap figure. Thus, any archer, whether he be average or expert, shooting a standard round can easily find the handicap equivalent for his score. This figure is reduced as the archer's performance improves. With a handicap figure available, an allowance can be allocated to an archer so that he can compete on an equal basis against archers of a higher or lower standard. It will be apparent that the lower the standard of the

92

Many archers find the use of binoculars a help in identifying their own shots, enabling critical aiming corrections to be made arrow by arrow.

archer, the greater will be his handicap allowance. Many tournament and club fixtures include awards based on handicapped scores, which means that you are neither penalized by being a poor shot nor would you have a special advantage by being an expert.

COACHING

The National Coaching Organization in the U.K. provides a first-class voluntary service for training archers at all levels. Many clubs include members who are Instructors, and there are County and Regional Coaches who look after the needs of the wider membership of archery clubs. Special archery weekends and other fixtures are frequently arranged, and, if you can participate in any session which is being run by a trained Instructor or Coach, you will benefit by his or her expert guidance. Every archer at one time or another needs extra help with his shooting and encouragement to better his own performance, but the secret of good shooting is in your own determination to improve and constant repetition of all the principles of the proper techniques.

Appendix A

TARGET ROUNDS

Name of Round	Number of arrows						
	100 yds	80 yds	60 yds	50 yds	40 yds	30 yds	20 yds
York	72	48	24				
St George	36	36	36				
New Western	48	48					
New National	48	24					
Hereford (Bristol I)		72	48	24			
Long Western		48	48				
Long National		48	24				
Albion		36	36	36			
Windsor			36	36	36		
American			30	30	30		
Western			48	48			
National			48	24			

Junior rounds

Name of Round	100 yds	80 yds	60 yds	50 yds	40 yds	30 yds	20 yds
Bristol I		72	48	24			
Bristol II			72	48	24		
Bristol III				72	48	24	
Bristol IV					72	48	24
Short Windsor				36	36	36	
St Nicholas					48	36	

Metric rounds

	90m	70m	60m	50m	40m	30m	20m	10m
FITA (Gentlemen)	36	36		36		36		
FITA (Ladies) (Metric I)		36	36	36		36		
Long Metric (Gentlemen)	36	36						
Long Metric (Ladies)		36	36					
Short Metric				36		36		

Junior rounds

	90m	70m	60m	50m	40m	30m	20m	10m
Metric I		36	36	36		36		
Metric II			36	36	36	36		
Metric III				36	36	36	36	
Metric IV					36	36	36	36

Indoor rounds

	20yds	30m	25m	18m
Portsmouth (60cm target face)	60			
Worcester (40cm target face)	60			
Stafford (80cm target face)		72		
FITA Round I (40cm target face)				30
FITA Round II (60cm target face)			30	

Notes

(*a*) In every round the longer or longest distance is shot first, and the shorter or shortest distance last.

(*b*) When FITA and Metric rounds are shot, FITA Rules apply.

(*c*) A FITA round may be shot in one day or over two consecutive days.

(*d*) All other rounds to be shot in one day (except in the case of a championship of more than one day's duration).

Appendix B   USEFUL ADDRESSES

Grand National Archery Society
Secretary: Mr J. J. Bray, National Agricultural Centre, Stoneleigh, Kenilworth, CU8 2LG, England

Association for Archery in Schools
Secretary: Mr S. E. Crisp, Rangemoor, Lytchett Matravers, Poole, Dorset, England

National Coaching Organiser
Mr Ellis Shepherd, 4 Park Drive, Rhyl, Clwyd, LL18 4DB, Wales

National Association of Archery Coaches
Mr W. H. West, 53 Worrell Avenue, Arnold, Notts, NG5 7GN, England

National Film Library
Mr J Adams, 132 Hapstead Hall Road, Hadsworth Wood, Birmingham 20, England

Society of Archer-Antiquaries
Secretary: Mr M. J. Weatherley, 18 Burlington Road, Birkdale, Southport, Lancs., England

BRITISH ARCHER (Published bi-monthly)
Technical Indexes Ltd, East Hampstead Road, Bracknell, Berks RG12 1NS, England

Archery Association for Australia
Mr F. Gavin, 22 London Drive, West Wollongong, 2500 New South Wales, Australia

Federation of Canadian Archers
Mrs C. Rohringer, Box 151, St Norbent, Manitoba, Canada

National Archery Association of the United States
Mr C. B. Shenk, 1951 Geraldson Drive, Lancaster, Pennsylvania, 17601, U.S.A.

Fédération Internationale de Tir à l'Arc
Mr D. M. Thomson, 46 The Balk, Walton, Wakefield, WF2 6JU, England